To Soror Pia –
Thanks so much
your support!
Konya

Sugar Plum
confections

Delicious Desserts to Satisfy Your Sweet Tooth

by

Konya Lindsey

Photographs by Steve Buchanan
Food Styling by Harry McMann

Acknowledgments

This book is the culmination of a long-awaited vision to bring delicious homemade desserts to the masses, and it could not have happened without the help of so many people.

First and foremost, I thank God, with whom all things are possible.

Steve Buchanan, for truly capturing the essence of what this book is about through your magnificent photography style.

Harry McMann, my food stylist, whose eye for detail is amazing.

Peter Quinn, for your graphic design expertise.

Kim Clarke, my hand model, for your friendship and support.

Sabrina Williams, for helping me share my story with the world.

My husband, Rahsaan, who tasted every single recipe that made it into this book — and even tasted the ones that didn't!

My sister, Leslie, who finally came around. Your advice and contributions to this book are immeasurable.

All my resident taste testers for your honest feedback and magnificent taste buds — especially the ER staff at Greater Baltimore Medical Center. You guys are the best!

And finally, a huge thank you to my circle of friends and family. Your support and encouragement has been my leaning post.

Library of Congress Control Number: 2008900385
ISBN: Softcover 978-1-4363-1710-8 Hardcover 978-1-4363-1711-5

This book was printed in the United States of America.

To order additional copies of this book, contact:
Xlibris Corporation
1-888-795-4274
www.Xlibris.com
Orders@Xlibris.com

Dedicated To

Rahsaan Lindsey
Thank you, my dear husband, for being my biggest fan.

Leslie Anderson
Thank you for sharing your love of baking with me, and for being the wonderful sister that you are.

the late Fannie Mae Coleman
Thank you, grandma, for first planting the seed.

Introduction

I have always had a passion for food – especially desserts. Being born into a family with deep Southern roots, I developed a pretty strong sweet tooth early on. Anyone who knows me can attest to the fact that I would take a good dessert over a meal any day.

As a young child, I can remember sitting in my grandmother's kitchen while she whipped up one of her famous cakes or pies and begging to lick the batter from the beaters! Smelling all the wonderful spices and aromas that came out of her kitchen was like heaven to me. While I was growing up, my family made sure I knew my way around a kitchen at an early age. I even remember helping my sister prepare homemade chocolate chip cookies and rice cereal treats every night so that I could sell them the next day at school. But it wasn't until later in life that I discovered how much I truly enjoyed cooking and baking – and the sense of pride and accomplishment I felt in seeing others enjoy the food that I prepared with my own hands.

Although I love to cook, baking has always held a special place in my heart. For me, it's almost therapeutic, even. Nothing puts me in a better mood than enjoying a delicious homemade piece of cake after a meal, or taking in the aroma of a pie fresh out of the oven. Over the years, however, I have encountered so many people who find baking to be such an extremely daunting and stressful task. It was because of this that I felt the need to write this cookbook. I want to help those who view baking as a chore to discover the joys in turning a simple, easy-to-follow recipe into a delicious confection that can be shared and enjoyed with family and friends. Although there may be quite a bit of detail involved – precise measurements, the right blend of quality ingredients, and proper preparation and baking techniques – baking can absolutely be fun and stress free!

The recipes in this book are reminiscent of all those wonderful desserts my family and I grew up on – from the Southern-style Hummingbird Cake inspired by my grandmother, to my classic apple pie that my husband looks forward to every apple-picking season, to the luscious peach cobbler that has everyone swooning during the holidays. The recipes are straightforward, easy to follow, and include natural, real ingredients (none of the artificial stuff, folks!). I've also included some additional tips and advice that I believe you'll find helpful as you try these recipes in your own home.

Now, I would be remiss if I didn't talk to you a little about moderation and discipline when it comes to these decadent recipes. I don't claim to be a health expert, but I do recognize the importance of maintaining a healthy lifestyle that incorporates a good, balanced diet and plenty of exercise. Splurging a bit every now and then is certainly okay by me, but just remember that as you indulge in the desserts in this cookbook, I encourage you to use moderation and share them with family and friends. It's much more fun that way!

It is my sincere hope that you enjoy all the recipes in this book as much as I do. For more information, questions, or comments, please check out my website at www.sugarplum-confections.com.

Here's to satisfying your sweet tooth!

Table of Contents

DESSERT BASICS

Key Equipment
Key Ingredients
Equivalent Weights & Measures
Substitutions

Dessert Basics: Key Equipment

In order to achieve successful, consistent results from any recipe, it all starts with the right ingredients and equipment. Here are some staple items I believe every baker needs in his or her kitchen to get the job done. As you try the recipes throughout this book, you will find you'll use these items over and over again.

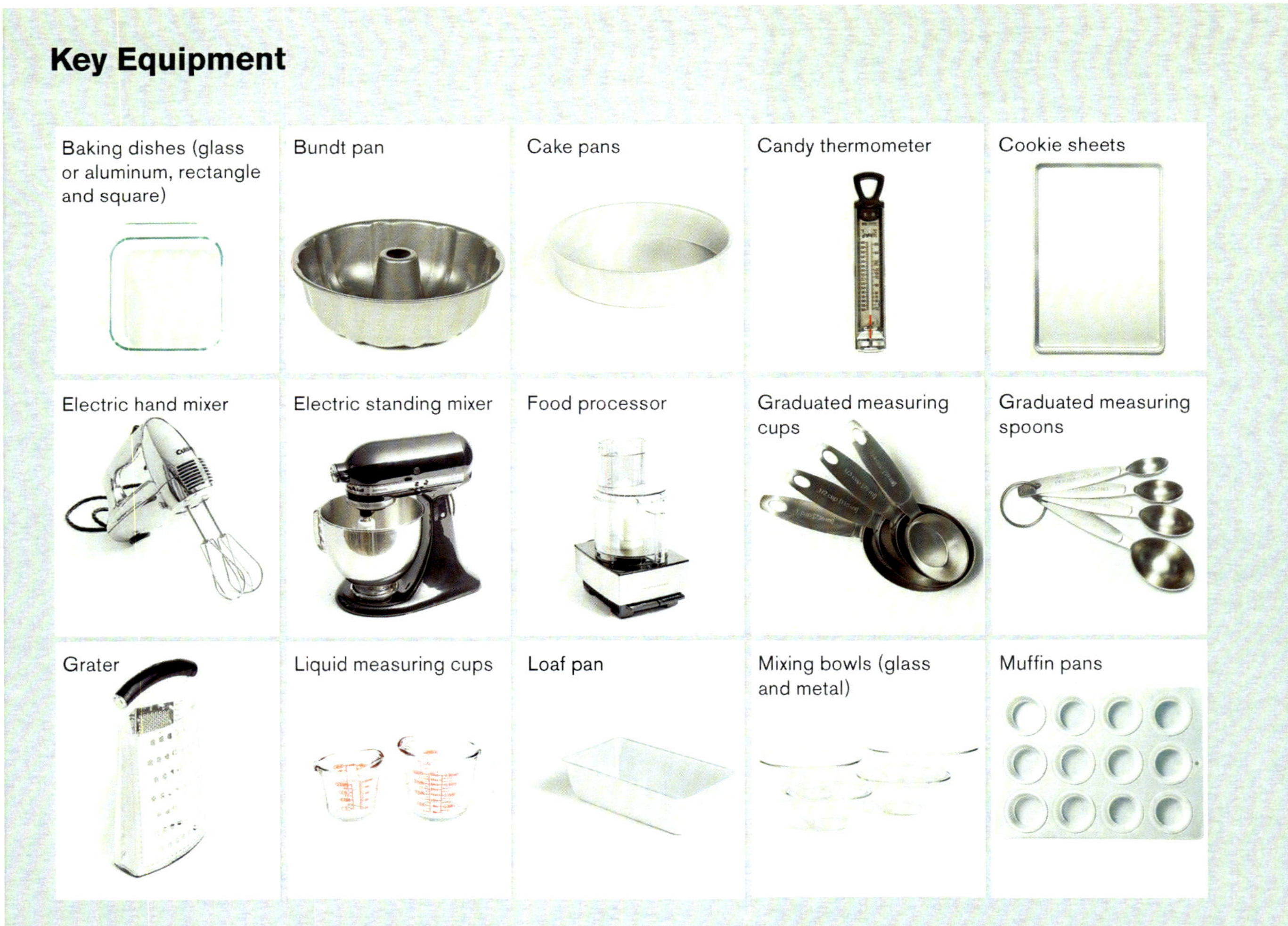

Pastry blender
Pastry brush
Pie pans
Rolling pin
Rubber spatulas
Sifter
Sifter/Sieve
Spatulas
Springform pan (with removable bottom)
Tart pan (with removable bottom)
Tube/Angel Food pan (w/ removable bottom)
Whisks
Wire cooling rack
Wooden spoons
Zester

Dessert Basics: Key Ingredients

Here are a list of ingredients that every baker should regularly stock in his or her kitchen and pantry. You can find them all right in your neighborhood grocery store.

Key Ingredients

All-Purpose Flour
Baking Powder (double-acting)
Baking Soda
Butter
Buttermilk
Cake Flour
Chocolate (bittersweet, milk, semisweet, unsweetened, cocoa powder, Dutch-processed cocoa powder)
Citrus Fruits (oranges, lemons, limes)
Cream of Tartar
Eggs (Note: All recipes in this book have been tested using large eggs)
Extracts (vanilla, lemon, almond)
Heavy Cream
Milk
Nuts (walnuts, almonds, pecans, etc.)
Oil (vegetable or canola)
Pastry Bag and Tips (A disposable plastic zip-top storage bag works well too!)
Salt (I use Kosher.)
Shortening
Sugar (brown, granulated, powdered)

Dessert Basics: Equivalent Weights and Measures

Measurement	Equals
Dash	Less than ⅛ teaspoon
1 ½ teaspoons	½ tablespoon
3 teaspoons	1 tablespoon
2 tablespoons	⅛ cup or 1 fluid ounce
4 tablespoons	¼ cup
5 tablespoons plus 1 teaspoon	⅓ cup
8 tablespoons	½ cup
12 tablespoons	¾ cup
16 tablespoons	1 cup
1 cup	8 fluid ounces
2 cups	1 pint or 16 fluid ounces
4 cups	1 quart or 32 fluid ounces
4 quarts	1 gallon
16 ounces	1 pound

Dessert Basics: Substitutions

Every now and then, you may be all ready to bake, only to find that you are missing one key ingredient! Here are some substitutions that I have found to be very helpful in a pinch:

Ingredient	Substitution
Baking Powder, 1 teaspoon	¼ teaspoon baking soda plus ½ teaspoon cream of tartar
Buttermilk, 1 cup	1 tablespoon vinegar OR lemon juice, plus enough milk to make 1 cup (let stand for 5–10 minutes) 1 cup plain yogurt 1 cup sour cream
Milk Chocolate, 1 ounce	1 ounce bittersweet or semisweet plus 1 tablespoon granulated sugar
Unsweetened Chocolate, 1 ounce	3 tablespoons unsweetened cocoa powder plus 1 tablespoon unsalted butter, shortening, or vegetable oil
Heavy Cream, 1 cup	⅔ cup whole milk plus ⅓ cup melted unsalted butter
Egg, 1 large whole	2 large egg yolks plus 1 tablespoon water 3½ tablespoons egg substitute
Egg Yolks, 2 large	1 large whole egg
Vanilla Extract, 1 teaspoon	½ vanilla bean, split and seeded
Unsalted Butter, ½ cup	½ cup margarine ½ cup solid vegetable shortening
Cake Flour, 1 cup	¾ cup all-purpose flour plus 2 tablespoons cornstarch
All-Purpose Flour, 1 cup	1 cup plus 2 tablespoons sifted cake flour
Whole Milk, 1 cup	1 cup low-fat milk ½ cup evaporated milk OR condensed milk plus ½ cup water 1 cup skim milk plus 2 tablespoons melted butter or margarine

TIPS FOR BAKING SUCCESS

Tips For Baking Success

Here are some tips and tidbits that will help as you navigate your way throughout this cookbook.

BAKING TIMES – Each recipe specifies a range of baking time; however, everyone's oven is different. Use the time range given in each recipe as a general guideline – the actual time it takes for your dessert to finish baking may be a little longer or shorter. As your recipe nears the end of the specified baking time, check for doneness often. Cakes and muffins are generally done when the top feels firm when lightly touched or when a toothpick or wooden skewer inserted into the center comes out clean. Pies and tarts are generally done when the center is set and the filling jiggles slightly when the pan is gently shaken (for fruit pies, you will see the filling start to thicken and bubble). Cookies and bars are generally done when the edges are slightly brown and the center is set. I have reduced the baking times for recipes like the Fudgy Brownies, Chocolate Chip Cookies and Oatmeal Cranberry Cookies by a minute or two so that they are slightly underbaked to maintain their chewy texture. If you prefer a slightly drier or crispier cookie, it's okay to increase the baking time by an additional 1 or 2 minutes.

BEATING AND MIXING – Several recipes in the book will instruct you to beat a mixture until "light and fluffy". This means you will need to blend the mixture rapidly by incorporating as much air as possible until the mixture is smooth, slightly thickened, and somewhat lighter in color *(Figure 1).*

Figure 1

Depending on what is specified in each recipe, you may use a handheld or standing electric mixer, spoon or whisk to do this. This step is especially important for most of the cake recipes in this book, as beating the butter, sugar and eggs together helps to develop its structure and texture. Each recipe will give you a timeframe for how long you are to beat the batter. Always be sure to stop the mixer periodically to scrape down the sides and bottom of the bowl. This will ensure your batter is well mixed.

Once the butter, eggs, and sugar are thoroughly beaten, the purpose of additional mixing is to blend in the remaining ingredients until they are just incorporated. Unless directed otherwise, most of the cake recipes will instruct you to alternate adding in the dry ingredients (flour mixture) and liquid ingredients (milk, buttermilk, etc.). I usually do this by adding the dry ingredients in 3 additions and the liquid ingredients in 2 additions, starting and ending with the dry ingredients. You'll want to do this fairly quickly with the electric mixer on low speed, being careful not to overmix the batter.

CITRUS ZEST – When zesting citrus fruits (lemons, oranges, limes, etc.), be sure to grate only the colored part of the rind. The white part of the rind (called the pith) is bitter. The zest is where the essential oils are in the fruit, which can add a wonderful flavor and aroma to your recipe.

DOUBLE BOILING – Some recipes in this book will instruct you to use this method for gently melting chocolate or cooking egg yolks. Place a heatproof, nonreactive bowl –either glass or stainless steel –snugly over a saucepan of gently simmering water. Be careful not to allow the water to touch the bottom of the bowl.

EGGS – All recipes in this book have been tested using large eggs. When a recipe calls for eggs to be separated, it is best to do this while the eggs are cold. To separate, gently crack the egg over a bowl. Using the tips of your thumbs, gently open the shell in half, allowing the whites to fall into the bowl while the yolk remains in the shell. Place the yolk in a separate bowl.

FATS – I use unsalted butter, shortening and vegetable or canola oil. Margarine would work as well, but avoid "butter spreads" or "whipped" butter or margarines. For the Basic Buttercream frosting, I sometimes use shortening in place of the butter to achieve a whiter color. For milk, I use whole milk in these recipes. I have found that low-fat or soy milk will also work fine, but using nonfat milk does not give your finished recipe the desired flavor or texture needed.

FOLDING – This means to incorporate an aerated substance (like beaten egg whites or whipped cream) into a heavier substance (like cake batter). It is best to use a rubber spatula to do this, so that the mixture will not deflate, but retain its volume and lightness. Using the rubber spatula, cut into the mixture *(Figure 1)* and gently turn the spatula over *(Figure 2)*, rotating the bowl after each turn *(Figure 3)*:

Figure 1

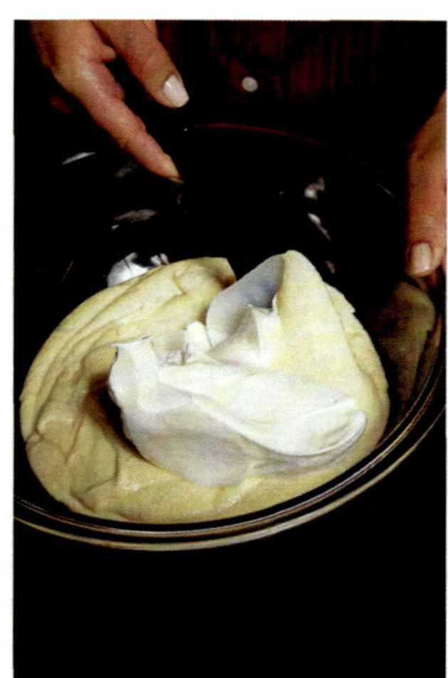

Figure 2

Figure 3

INGREDIENTS – Be sure to review the recipe before you start, to ensure you have all the necessary ingredients. Unless otherwise specified in the recipe, I recommend that you start with room temperature ingredients. This includes eggs, butter, milk, buttermilk, sour cream and shortening. To bring these items to room temperature, allow them to sit out on the counter for about 30 minutes before you begin. This will ensure all your ingredients will be well incorporated and your finished product achieves its desired structure and texture.

MEASURING – Use measuring cups or measuring spoons to accurately measure dry ingredients. To measure dry ingredients (e.g., flour), spoon into measuring cup and level off with the flat end of a knife. Avoid dipping the cup into the container as this packs the contents down and can throw off your desired measurement. For liquids, use a glass measuring cup or measuring spoons. When using a measuring cup, set the cup on the counter before filling, and check the measurement at eye level for accuracy. Some recipes may call for an ingredient to be "divided" (example: 2 cups of granulated sugar, divided) – this simply means that as you prepare the recipe, a portion of that ingredient may be used during one step, while the remaining portion will be used in another step later on in the recipe.

PASTRY CRUSTS AND SHELLS – When making pie crusts or tart pastry shells, be sure that the butter or shortening called for in the recipe is cold. This will ensure a lighter, flakier crust. Use a fork or pastry cutter to incorporate the butter or shortening into the flour until the mixture resembles coarse meal – this is also referred to as "cutting in". Be sure not to handle the dough too much – overmixing can cause the gluten in the flour to develop, resulting in a heavy, tough crust. Be sure to roll out your dough on a lightly floured surface. Start from the center and roll out toward the end of the dough, rotating the dough periodically to ensure it does not stick to the surface.

PREHEATING YOUR OVEN – You cannot miss this step! Before you bake, it is very important to give your oven time to reach the correct temperature. Place the oven rack in the center of the oven, and allow 10–15 minutes of preheating time. If you are baking only one pan, place it in the center of the rack to ensure even baking. If you are baking more than one pan at a time, space the pans evenly apart so that they are not touching each other or the sides of the oven.

PREP TIMES – Each recipe shows an "Active Prep" time frame, which includes the time necessary to mix and bake each specified dessert from start to finish. The recipes will also display an "Inactive Prep" timeframe, which is the additional unattended time required for steps such as freezing, chilling, or cooling.

PREPARING BAKING PANS – Many of the recipes in this book call for you to grease (or grease and flour) the baking pan(s) to prevent any sticking. Butter, shortening, or nonstick cooking sprays are all great options. To flour the pan, place 1–2 teaspoons of flour in the pan after you have greased it and gently shake it from side to side until the bottom and sides are covered. Discard any excess flour. Baking sprays that have flour included (such as Baker's Joy) will also work just as well. For muffins, you may also use paper or foil liners instead. When filling the pans, be sure to pour the same amount of batter into each cake or muffin pan to ensure they all bake evenly.

SIFTING – This is a very important step! Most of the recipes in this book with instruct you to sift your dry ingredients (flour, salt, baking powder, etc.) prior to adding them to the wet ingredients. For certain cakes, you will even be instructed to sift the flour prior to measuring. This is done to remove any hard particles or granules that may be in there, and to also incorporate air into the flour –producing a light, tender cake.

WHIPPING – When whipping ingredients like egg whites or heavy cream, use either a whisk or an electric mixer fitted with a whisk attachment. Egg whites whip best when they are at room temperature. To achieve maximum volume, make sure your bowl and beaters are thoroughly clean and that there is absolutely no yolk in the whites. If there is any type of fat in the bowl, your whites will not whip up to your desired volume. When whipping heavy cream, make sure the cream, bowl, and beaters are cold. If you have the time, set your bowl and beaters in the freezer for 5–10 minutes beforehand. See illustrations below for determining whether your mixture has achieved soft peaks or stiff peaks:

soft peak

stiff peak

CAKES

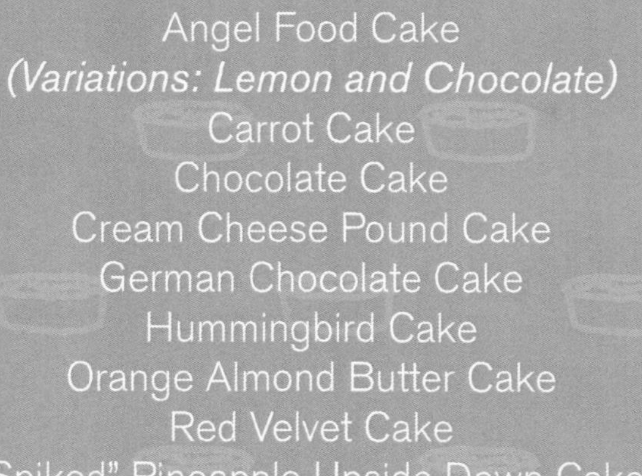

Angel Food Cake

This light and airy cake contains absolutely no fat. Serve a slice with some fresh berries and enjoy a "heavenly" after-dinner treat!

1. Preheat oven to 350°F. Place sugar in an electric food processor and blend until superfine, about 30 seconds. In a medium bowl, sift together presifted cake flour, 3/4 cup of sugar, and salt. Set aside.
2. Using an electric mixer on medium speed, whip egg whites in a large bowl until foamy, about 30 seconds. Add in cream of tartar and continue to beat on medium speed until soft peaks form, about 2–3 minutes. Gradually add in remaining 1 cup of sugar, adding 1/4 cup at a time, until stiff peaks form and whites become shiny. Add in vanilla extract.
3. Gradually add the flour mixture into the egg white mixture, about 1/4 cup at a time, by sifting the flour mixture over the egg white mixture and gently folding it in using a large rubber spatula. Be careful not to overmix the batter or the egg whites will deflate.
4. Pour the batter into ungreased 10-inch tube pan with a removable bottom –the pan will almost be filled to the top. Run a thin knife through the batter to remove any air pockets or bubbles, and then gently smooth the top. Bake for about 40–45 minutes, or until a wooden skewer inserted into the cake comes out clean. The cake will have risen considerably and the top of the cake will have some cracks. Once cake is removed from the oven, immediately turn the pan upside down and place the inner tube on the top of a wine or soda bottle. Cool upside down in pan, at least 2 hours. When cake is completely cooled, run a thin knife around the sides and the bottom of the pan to remove. Transfer to a serving plate.

makes

12 to 15 servings

Active Prep: 1 hour

Inactive Prep: 2 hours

ingredients

1 3/4 cups granulated sugar, divided
1 cup sifted cake flour
1/2 teaspoon salt
16 large egg whites, room temperature (approximately 2 cups)
2 teaspoons cream of tartar
2 teaspoons vanilla extract

Chocolate Angel Food Cake (variation): Prepare flour mixture and beaten egg whites as directed. In a small bowl, combine 4 tablespoons of Dutch-processed cocoa powder (do not use regular unsweetened cocoa powder), 1 heaping teaspoon of instant espresso powder, and 1/4 cup of boiling water. Stir until smooth. Add in vanilla extract. After beating the egg whites as directed, remove one cup of the beaten egg whites and whisk into the cocoa powder mixture to lighten. Set aside. Add the flour mixture into remaining egg whites as directed. Gently fold in cocoa powder mixture until well incorporated, being careful not to overmix. Pour batter into tube pan and bake as directed.

Lemon Angel Food Cake (variation): Prepare flour mixture and beaten egg whites as directed. Once flour mixture had been added to egg whites as directed, gently fold in 2 tablespoons of lemon juice and 2 teaspoons of grated lemon zest until well incorporated, being careful not to overmix. Pour batter into tube pan and bake as directed.

Recipe Tip: For an extra treat, drizzle a little Simple Sugar Glaze (see recipe) on top of cake before serving.

Carrot Cake

The nuts, raisins, and coconut lend a hearty texture to this old-fashioned favorite. You'll enjoy every mouthful!

makes

10 to 12 servings

Active Prep: 1 hour

Inactive Prep: 30 minutes

ingredients

2 cups all-purpose flour
1 1/2 teaspoons baking powder
1 teaspoon baking soda
1 teaspoon salt
2 teaspoons cinnamon
1/2 teaspoon nutmeg
3/4 cup granulated sugar
3/4 cup light brown sugar, firmly packed
3/4 cup unsalted butter, softened
2 large eggs
2 teaspoons vanilla extract
1/2 cup buttermilk
2 cups grated carrots (about 2–3 large carrots)
3/4 cup chopped walnuts or pecans (optional)
1/2 cup raisins (optional)
1/2 cup coconut (optional)
Cream Cheese Frosting (see recipe)

1. Preheat oven to 350°F. Grease and flour two 8- or 9-inch cake pans. Set aside.

2. In a medium bowl, sift together flour, baking powder, baking soda, salt, cinnamon, and nutmeg. Set aside.

3. Using an electric mixer on medium speed, beat granulated sugar, brown sugar and butter in a large bowl until light and fluffy, about 2–3 minutes. Add in eggs and vanilla extract and mix until well combined. With mixer on low, add in flour mixture alternately with the buttermilk, beginning and ending with the flour mixture. Mix until just combined. Fold in carrots, nuts, raisins, and coconut. Stop the mixer to scrape down the sides of the bowl as needed.

4. Pour batter evenly into prepared pans. Bake for about 25–30 minutes, or until toothpick inserted in the center of each cake layer out clean. Cool in pans for about 20 minutes, then transfer onto a cooling rack. Allow cakes to cool completely before frosting.

5. To assemble cake, place one cake layer on a plate. Using an offset spatula, evenly spread 1 cup of frosting on the top. Place the second cake layer on top of the first, stacking the layers as evenly as possible. Spread the remaining frosting over the top and sides of the cake. Refrigerate for 20 minutes before serving.

Chocolate Cake

Chocoholics, beware! This cake is moist, delicious, and is sure to satisfy your craving. Adding coffee to the batter enhances the richness of the cake and fully brings out its wonderful chocolate flavor.

12 to 15 servings

Active Prep: 1 hour

Inactive Prep: 30 minutes

ingredients

3 eggs
¾ cup vegetable oil
1½ cups buttermilk
1½ teaspoons vanilla extract
2½ cups all-purpose flour
2¾ cups granulated sugar
1½ cups unsweetened cocoa powder
2½ teaspoons baking soda
1¼ teaspoons baking powder
1¼ teaspoons salt
1½ cups hot brewed coffee
Milk Chocolate Frosting (see recipe)

1. Preheat oven to 350°F. Grease and flour three 8- or 9-inch cake pans. Set aside.

2. In a medium bowl, whisk together eggs, vegetable oil, buttermilk, and vanilla extract until smooth and well combined. Set aside.

3. In a large bowl, sift together flour, sugar, cocoa powder, baking soda, baking powder, and salt. Using an electric mixer on low speed, slowly add egg mixture to the flour mixture until well incorporated. Stir in hot coffee until just combined. Stop the mixer to scrape down the sides of the bowl as needed.

4. Pour batter evenly into prepared pans. Bake for about 30–35 minutes, or until toothpick inserted in the center of each cake layer out clean. Cool in pans for about 20 minutes, then transfer onto a cooling rack. Allow cakes to cool completely before frosting.

5. To assemble cake, place one cake layer on a plate. Using an offset spatula, evenly spread 1 cup of frosting on the top. Place the second cake layer on top of the first, stacking the layers as evenly as possible, and spread another cup of frosting on the top. Place the last layer on the top, pressing down lightly on all three layers to secure. Spread the remaining frosting over the top and sides of the cake. Refrigerate for 20 minutes before serving.

Cream Cheese Pound Cake

Although this rich, moist cake is perfect all on its own, I love to serve it with fresh berries and sweetened whipped cream.

10 to 12 servings

Active Prep: 1 ½ hours

Inactive Prep: 30 minutes

ingredients

3 cups all-purpose flour

½ teaspoon salt

1 ½ cups unsalted butter, softened

1 8-oz. package cream cheese, softened

3 cups sugar

6 eggs

1 ½ teaspoons vanilla extract

¼ teaspoon almond extract

1 heaping teaspoon grated orange zest

1. Preheat oven to 300°F. Grease and flour a 10-inch tube pan with a removable bottom. Set aside.

2. In a medium bowl, sift together flour, and salt. Set aside.

3. Using an electric mixer on medium speed, cream butter and cream cheese in a large bowl until well combined, about 2–3 minutes. Add sugar and mix another 3 minutes until light and fluffy. Add in eggs, one at a time, until well combined. Add in vanilla and almond extracts. With mixer on low, gradually add in flour mixture until just combined. Be careful not to overmix. Stop the mixer to scrape down the sides of the bowl as needed. Fold in orange zest.

4. Pour batter into prepared tube pan and smooth the top. Bake for about 1 hour and 30 minutes, or until a wooden skewer inserted into the cake comes out clean. Cool in pan for 20 minutes, then transfer to a cooling rack. Cake can be served warm or at room temperature.

German Chocolate Cake

This stunning cake is both rich and indulgent. A perfect choice for any special occasion.

1. Preheat oven to 350°F. Grease and flour three 8- or 9-inch cake pans. Set aside.
2. In a small microwaveable bowl, combine chocolate, coffee powder, and water. Microwave on high for 1 minute, or until chocolate is almost melted. Remove from microwave and stir until mixture is smooth and chocolate is completely melted. Set aside.
3. In a medium bowl, sift together all-purpose flour, cake flour, baking soda, baking powder and salt. Set aside.
4. In another medium bowl, beat the four egg whites using an electric mixer until stiff peaks form. Set aside.
5. Using an electric mixer on medium speed, cream butter and sugar in a large bowl until light and fluffy, about 2–3 minutes. Add in the four egg yolks, one at a time, and mix until well combined. Add in chocolate mixture and vanilla extract. With mixer on low, add in flour mixture alternately with buttermilk, beginning and ending with the flour mixture. Mix until just combined. Stop the mixer to scrape down the sides of the bowl as needed.
6. Using a rubber spatula, gently fold the beaten egg whites into cake batter. Be careful not to overmix. Pour batter evenly into prepared pans. Bake for about 25–30 minutes, or until toothpick inserted in the center of each cake comes out clean. Cool in pans for 20 minutes, then transfer onto a cooling rack. Allow cakes to cool completely before frosting.
7. To assemble cake, place the first layer on cake plate. Using an offset spatula, evenly spread one-third of the Toasted Pecan-Coconut Frosting on the top. Place the second cake layer on top, stacking the layers as evenly as possible. Spread another third of the frosting over the top. Place the last layer on the top, pressing down lightly on all three layers to secure. Spread the remaining frosting over the top of the cake. Refrigerate cake for 20–30 minutes before serving.

makes

12 to 15 servings

Active Prep: 1 hour

Inactive Prep: 1 hour

ingredients

4 ounces German's sweet chocolate
1 teaspoon instant coffee powder
½ cup water
1 cup all-purpose flour
1 cup cake flour
1 teaspoon baking soda
½ teaspoon baking powder
½ teaspoon salt
4 eggs, separated
1 cup unsalted butter, softened
1 ½ cups granulated sugar
1 teaspoon vanilla extract
1 cup buttermilk
Toasted Pecan-Coconut Frosting
(see recipe)

Hummingbird Cake

This delicious spice cake is my take on an old Southern favorite. Ripe, sweet bananas and juicy pineapple lend to the cake's moist and tender texture.

12 to 15 servings

Active Prep: 1 hour

Inactive Prep: 1 hour

ingredients

3 eggs
1 ½ cups vegetable oil
2 teaspoons vanilla extract
3 cups all-purpose flour
2 cups granulated sugar
2 teaspoons baking soda
2 heaping teaspoons ground cinnamon
¾ teaspoon salt
1 cup (8 oz. can) crushed pineapple, with juice
2 cups chopped pecans, divided
2 cups mashed bananas (about 3–4 large bananas)
Cream Cheese Frosting (see recipe)

1. Preheat oven to 350°F. Grease and flour three 8- or 9-inch cake pans. Set aside.
2. In a small bowl, whisk together eggs, vegetable oil, and vanilla extract until well combined. Set aside.
3. In a large bowl, sift together flour, sugar, baking soda, cinnamon, and salt. Mix in egg mixture by hand until well incorporated. Stir in pineapple and 1 cup pecans and mix until well combined. Fold in bananas.
4. Pour batter evenly into prepared pans. Bake for about 25 to 30 minutes, or until toothpick inserted in the center of each cake layer out clean. Cool in pans for 20 minutes, then transfer onto a cooling rack. Allow cakes to cool completely before frosting.
5. To assemble cake, place one cake layer on a plate. Using an offset spatula, evenly spread 1 cup of frosting on the top. Place the second cake layer on top of the first, stacking the layers as evenly as possible, and spread another cup of frosting on the top. Place the last layer on the top, pressing down lightly on all three layers to secure. Spread the remaining frosting over the top and sides of the cake. Use remaining 1 cup of pecans to decorate the sides of the cake. Refrigerate for 20 minutes before serving.

Orange Almond Butter Cake

The almond and orange flavors in this cake are a match made in heaven. To keep it moist, orange syrup is poured over the cake while it's still warm. A thin orange glaze also complements the cake wonderfully.

10 to 12 servings

Active Prep: 1 hour

Inactive Prep: 30 minutes

ingredients

2 cups all-purpose flour
2 teaspoons baking powder
½ teaspoon baking soda
½ teaspoon salt
1 cup unsalted butter, softened
2 cups granulated sugar, divided
3 eggs
¾ teaspoon almond extract
1 teaspoon orange extract
1 cup buttermilk
3 tablespoons grated orange zest
½ cup orange juice
Orange Glaze (see recipe)
¼ cup sliced almonds, for garnishing

1. Preheat oven to 350°F. Grease and flour a 9- or 10-inch bundt pan. Set aside.

2. In a medium bowl, sift together flour, baking powder, baking soda and salt. Set aside.

3. Using an electric mixer on medium speed, beat butter in a large bowl until light and fluffy, about 2–3 minutes. Scrape down the sides of the bowl and beat for an additional 2 minutes. Gradually add in 1½ cups of sugar, ¼ cup at a time, beating for 1 minute after each addition. Add eggs, one at a time, beating well after each addition. Mix in almond and orange extracts. With mixer on low, add the flour mixture and buttermilk alternately, starting and ending with the flour mixture. Mix until just combined. Stop the mixer to scrape down the sides of the bowl as needed. Fold in orange zest.

4. Pour batter evenly into prepared cake pan and smooth the top. Bake for about 40–45 minutes or until a wooden skewer inserted into the cake comes out clean. While cake is in the oven, combine orange juice and remaining ½ cup of sugar in a small saucepan. Bring to a simmer over medium high heat, stirring constantly until all the sugar is dissolved. Remove from heat and pour into a glass measuring cup. Set aside to cool.

5. Remove cake from oven and cool in pan for 10 minutes. Place a cooling rack over a sheet pan. Invert cake onto cooling rack. Slowly pour entire orange juice mixture evenly onto warm cake, allowing the cake to absorb the entire mixture *(Figure 1)*. Once cake is completely cooled, drizzle Orange Glaze over cake and sprinkle top with almonds.

Recipe Tip: For a more intense almond flavor, toast the sliced almonds before garnishing the cake. Place almonds in a dry skillet over medium low heat, stirring occasionally, until slightly browned.

Figure 1

Red Velvet Cake

Rich red cake layers contrast against a wonderful white cream cheese frosting. This cake is a stunning ending to any meal.

1. Preheat oven to 350°F. Grease and flour two 8- or 9-inch cake pans. Set aside.
2. In a large bowl, sift together cake flour, cocoa, sugar, baking powder, baking soda, and salt. Set aside.
3. Using an electric mixer on medium speed, mix oil, buttermilk, eggs, vanilla extract, food coloring, and vinegar until well combined. Turn mixer down to low, and add in flour mixture. Mix just until all ingredients are incorporated and batter is smooth.
4. Pour batter evenly into prepared pans. Bake for about 30–35 minutes or until toothpick inserted in the center of each cake layer out clean. Cool in pans for 20 minutes, then transfer onto a cooling rack. Allow cakes to cool completely before frosting.
5. To assemble cake, place one cake layer on a plate. Using an offset spatula, evenly spread 1 cup of frosting on the top. Place the second cake layer on top of the first, stacking the layers as evenly as possible. Spread the remaining frosting over the top and sides of the cake. Refrigerate for 20 minutes before serving.

10 to 12 servings

Active Prep: 1½ hours

Inactive Prep: 1 hour

ingredients

3 cups cake flour
3 tablespoons unsweetened cocoa powder
1½ cups granulated sugar
1¾ teaspoons baking powder
1 teaspoon baking soda
1 teaspoon salt
2 cups vegetable oil
1 cup buttermilk
3 eggs
2 teaspoons vanilla extract
1 tablespoon red food coloring
2 teaspoons white vinegar
Cream Cheese Frosting (see recipe)

"Spiked" Pineapple Upside Down Cake

This perfect combination of sweet caramelized pineapple and moist butter cake is at its best when prepared the old-fashioned way —in a cast iron skillet. Serve it either warm or at room temperature.

10 to 12 servings

Active Prep: 1 hour

Inactive Prep: 20 minutes

ingredients

1 cup cake flour
1 cup all-purpose flour
1½ teaspoons baking powder
1 teaspoon baking soda
¼ teaspoon salt
½ cup, plus 4 tablespoons unsalted butter
¾ cup light or dark brown sugar
2 tablespoons Amaretto, or any almond-flavored liqueur
7 pineapple slices, drained
¼ cup pecans, coarsely chopped
7 maraschino cherries
1 cup granulated sugar
2 eggs
2 teaspoons vanilla extract
2 tablespoons bourbon whiskey
1 cup buttermilk

1. Preheat oven to 350°F. In a medium bowl, sift together cake flour, all-purpose flour, baking powder, baking soda, and salt. Set aside.

2. Using a 10- or 12-inch cast iron skillet, melt 4 tablespoons of butter over medium high heat. Using a wooden spoon, stir in brown sugar and cook until brown sugar is melted and mixture is bubbly, about 2 minutes. Add in Amaretto liqueur and cook for one more minute. Place pineapple slices in the bottom of the skillet (6 slices around the outside, 1 in the center), and cook for an additional 2 minutes. Turn pineapple slices over and remove from heat. Place a maraschino cherry in the center of each pineapple slice. Sprinkle pecans in the open spaces between the pineapple slices. Set aside.

3. Using an electric mixer on medium speed, cream remaining ½ cup of butter until light and fluffy, about 2–3 minutes. Add in granulated sugar, ¼ cup at a time, beating for 1 minute after each addition. Add eggs one at a time, beating well after each addition. Stir in vanilla extract and bourbon whiskey. With mixer on low, add the flour mixture and buttermilk alternately, starting and ending with the flour mixture. Mix until just combined. Stop the mixer to scrape down the sides of the bowl as needed.

4. Pour batter evenly over pineapple slices, covering all edges. Bake for about 35 minutes, or until toothpick inserted in the center comes out clean. Cool in the skillet on a cooling rack for 5 minutes. Run a thin knife around edges of the skillet and then carefully invert cake onto a plate, pineapple side up. Serve warm or at room temperature.

Recipe Tip: Don't have a cast iron skillet? Prepare pineapple slices as directed above in a sauté pan, then transfer to a greased and floured 9- or 10-inch cake pan. Add maraschino cherries and pecans as directed. Once you have prepared the cake batter, pour over pineapple slices and bake as directed.

White Cake

From birthdays to weddings, this cake is amazingly versatile. To get a slightly whiter cake, I use shortening instead of butter.

1. Separate egg yolks and whites, being careful not to get any yolks into the egg whites. Let whites stand at room temperature for 30 minutes.
2. Preheat oven to 350°F. Grease and flour a two 8- or 9-inch cake pans. Set aside.
3. In a medium bowl, sift together flour, baking powder, baking soda, and salt. Set aside.
4. In a large, clean bowl, whip egg whites until foamy, about 30 seconds. Add in cream of tartar and continue to whip until soft peaks form, about 1–2 minutes. Gradually add in ½ cup of sugar and continue to whip until whites are shiny and stiff peaks form, about 2–3 minutes. Set aside.
5. Using an electric mixer on medium speed, beat butter or shortening until light and fluffy, about 2–3 minutes. Scrape down the sides of the bowl and add in remaining 1¼ cups of sugar. Beat for an additional 2 minutes. Add in egg yolks, one at a time, beating for 30 seconds after each addition. Add vanilla extract and mix until well combined.
6. With mixer on low, add the flour mixture and buttermilk alternately, starting and ending with the flour mixture. Mix until just combined. Using a rubber spatula, gently fold in egg whites until just combined. Be careful not to overmix the batter or egg whites will deflate.
7. Pour batter evenly into prepared cake pans. Bake for about 25–30 minutes or until toothpick inserted in the center of each cake layer out clean. Cool in pans for 20 minutes, then transfer onto a cooling rack. Allow cakes to cool completely before frosting.
8. To assemble cake, place one cake layer on a plate. Using an offset spatula, evenly spread 1 cup of frosting on the top. Place the second cake layer on top of the first, stacking the layers as evenly as possible. Spread the remaining frosting over the top and sides of the cake. Refrigerate for 20 minutes before serving.

— makes —

10 to 12 servings

Active Prep: 1 hour
Inactive Prep: 1 hour

— ingredients —

- 4 eggs, separated
- 2 cups all-purpose flour
- 1½ teaspoons baking powder
- ½ teaspoon baking soda
- ½ teaspoon salt
- ¼ teaspoon cream of tartar
- ½ cup unsalted butter or shortening, softened
- 1¾ cups granulated sugar, divided
- 1½ teaspoons vanilla extract
- 1⅓ cups buttermilk
- Basic Buttercream Frosting (see recipe)

Recipe Tip: To get a slightly whiter cake, try using shortening instead of butter and clear vanilla extract.

PIES, TARTS AND COBBLERS

Deep-Dish Apple Pie
Fruit Tart
Key Lime Pie
Peach Cobbler
Sweet Potato Pie

Deep-Dish Apple Pie

With tart and sweet apples, aromatic spices, and a buttery, flaky crust, this old-fashioned deep-dish pie warms both your heart and home. Serve warm with a scoop of vanilla ice cream for an extra special treat.

8 to 10 servings

Active Prep: 1½ hours
Inactive Prep: 30 minutes

ingredients

- 6–7 medium baking apples (Granny Smith, Gala, McIntosh, or Pippin)
- 2 tablespoons lemon juice
- 1 cup granulated sugar, plus more for sprinkling
- 1 heaping teaspoon cinnamon
- ¼ teaspoon nutmeg
- ½ teaspoon salt
- ¼ cup all-purpose flour
- Double Crust Pie Pastry, unbaked (see recipe)
- 2 tablespoons unsalted butter or margarine
- egg wash (1 egg beaten with 1 tablespoon milk)

1. Preheat oven to 375°F. Prepare crust in an 8- or 9-inch pie pan, according to recipe. Set aside.

2. Peel, core, and slice apples, about ¼-inch thick. Place in medium bowl and toss with lemon juice to prevent browning. Add sugar, cinnamon, nutmeg, salt, and flour. Mix until well combined.

3. Pour apple filling into prepared bottom crust and dot the top with butter. Place second piece of rolled-out dough on top of filling. Trim and crimp edges to seal, using a fork or your fingers. Cut 3–4 half-inch slits in top of pie to allow steam to escape. Brush top lightly with egg wash and sprinkle lightly with sugar.

4. Place pie on a cookie sheet in case of spillage during baking. Bake for 45–55 minutes or until crust is golden brown and juices are thickened and bubbly. Allow to cool slightly before serving.

Recipe Tip: Try adding ½ cup of dried fruit (raisins, cherries, cranberries, etc.) to the apple mixture. Bake as directed above.

Fruit Tart

This dessert is pure elegance. A sweet pastry crust filled with rich and thick vanilla cream, then topped with fresh seasonal fruit.

— *makes* —

8 to 10 servings

Active Prep: 2 hours

Inactive Prep: 2-4 hours

— *ingredients* —

1/8 cup all-purpose flour
3 tablespoons cornstarch
3 egg yolks
1/4 cup granulated sugar
1 1/4 cups whole milk
1 vanilla bean, split lengthwise
1 tablespoon Amaretto, or any almond-flavored liqueur (optional)
Tart Pastry Crust, baked (see recipe)
Apricot Glaze (see recipe)
3 cups fresh fruit (strawberries, blue berries, blackberries, raspberries, bananas, pineapple, etc.)

1. Prepare pastry crust in a 9- or 10-inch tart pan with a removable bottom, according to recipe. Set aside.

2. In a small bowl, sift together flour and cornstarch. In a medium bowl, combine egg yolks and sugar using a wooden spoon. Add the flour mixture to the egg mixture and stir until mixture is smooth. Set aside.

3. In a small saucepan, combine milk and vanilla bean. Cook over medium high heat until milk comes to a simmer, about 5 minutes. Remove from heat and take out vanilla bean. While whisking constantly, slowly add hot milk to the egg mixture until thoroughly combined. Place mixture back into stove and cook over medium heat, whisking constantly until mixture becomes very thick, about 2–3 minutes. Remove from heat and whisk in Amaretto liqueur. Place mixture into a small bowl, cover tightly with plastic wrap and refrigerate until completely chilled, at least 2 hours.

4. To assemble tart, remove baked pastry crust from tart pan and transfer to a serving plate. Remove pastry cream from refrigerator and whisk vigorously until smooth. Set aside.

5. Using a pastry brush, spread a thin layer of Apricot Glaze over the bottom and sides of tart pastry crust. Slice fruit (if using blueberries, blackberries or raspberries, you may leave them whole). Using an offset spatula, spread cream evenly into prepared tart pastry crust. Arrange fruit in an overlapping pattern on top of pastry cream, making sure to cover as much of the cream as possible. Gently brush a thin layer of glaze onto the fruit. Refrigerate at least 1 hour before serving.

Recipe Tips: (1) For the pastry cream, if lumps occur while adding the hot milk to the egg yolk mixture, just strain mixture through a fine strainer to remove lumps before placing back into saucepan. (2) For the glaze, you can also use semisweet chocolate or a fruit preserves of your choice. You can also substitute the one tablespoon of water for a tablespoon of Grand Marnier or any other liqueur.

Key Lime Pie

This simple, refreshing dessert is sure to please any crowd. Garnish each slice with a generous dollop of sweetened whipped cream for a nice finish.

— makes —

8 to 10 servings

Active Prep: 45 minutes

Inactive Prep: 3-4 hours

— ingredients —

1 Graham Cracker Crust, unbaked (see recipe)

5 eggs yolks

20 oz. can (about 2½ cups) sweetened condensed milk

¾ cup key lime juice

1 tablespoon grated lime zest

1. Preheat oven to 350°F. Prepare crust in an 8- or 9-inch pie pan, according to recipe. Set aside.

2. In a medium bowl, whisk egg yolks until they become pale and thick, about 2–3 minutes. Whisking continuously, slowly add in sweetened condensed milk until well combined. Add lime juice and zest. Stir until mixture is well combined and slightly thickened.

3. Pour mixture into prepared pie crust. Bake for about 18–20 minutes, or until filling is set (do not allow filling to brown). Cool for 15 minutes, then refrigerate for at least 3–4 hours before serving.

Recipe Tip: If you cannot find key limes, you can use Persian limes, which are more readily available in your local grocery store.

Peach Cobbler

You'll enjoy my version of this down-home Southern favorite. Serve warm all by itself or with a generous scoop of vanilla ice cream.

— makes —

10 to 12 servings

Active Prep: 1 ½ hours

Inactive Prep: 30 minutes

— ingredients —

5 lbs. sliced peaches, fresh or frozen (not canned)

½ cup frozen apple juice concentrate, thawed

¼ cup unsalted butter

2 teaspoons cinnamon, plus more for sprinkling

1 teaspoon nutmeg

1 cup granulated sugar, plus more for sprinkling

1 cup light or dark brown sugar, firmly packed

3 heaping tablespoons all-purpose flour

Double Crust Pie Pastry, unbaked (see recipe)

2 tablespoons unsalted butter

egg wash (1 egg beaten with 1 tablespoon milk)

1. Preheat oven to 375°F. Prepare crust in a 9" x 13" pie pan, according to recipe. Set aside.

2. In a large saucepan, combine peaches, apple juice concentrate, butter, cinnamon, nutmeg, sugar, and brown sugar over medium low heat. Bring to a simmer and cook until peaches become tender, about 20–25 minutes.

3. Remove ½ cup of juices from the peach mixture and place in a small bowl. Using a whisk, gradually add in flour, whisking constantly until mixture is smooth. Slowly add in flour mixture back into peach mixture, stirring until thickened. Remove from heat and cool slightly.

4. Remove one of the pastry discs from refrigerator and allow to sit at room temperature for 5 minutes. On a floured surface, roll out the dough into a 12" x 15" rectangle. Transfer dough to 9" x 13" pan; lightly press the dough into the bottom and sides of the pan, using your fingers. Be careful not to stretch the dough. Pour peach filling into crust and dot the top with butter.

5. Remove second disc from refrigerator. Roll out the dough into a rectangle slightly larger than the pan. Place dough on top of filling. Trim and crimp edges to seal, using a fork or your fingers. Cut 3-4 half-inch slits in top of pie to allow steam to escape. Brush top lightly with egg wash and sprinkle lightly with sugar and cinnamon.

6. Place cobbler on a cookie sheet in case of spillage during baking. Bake in oven for 35–40 minutes or until crust is golden brown and juices are thickened and bubbly. Allow to cool slightly before serving.

Recipe Tip: For a nice decorative touch, roll the top crust out as directed. Using a sharp knife, cut dough into ½-inch strips. Place strips over filling in an overlapping pattern to make a lattice design. Trim and crimp edges to seal and continue with recipe as directed.

Sweet Potato Pie

Roasting the sweet potatoes really intensifies the flavor and texture of this old-school Southern dessert.

1. Preheat oven to 350°F. Prepare pie crust for an 8- or 9-inch pie pan, according to recipe. Set aside.
2. Using an electric hand mixer on medium speed, beat warm sweet potatoes and butter in a large bowl until thoroughly combined and mixture become smooth, about 3–4 minutes. Add cinnamon, nutmeg, salt, granulated sugar, brown sugar, vanilla extract, eggs, milk, orange zest, lemon juice, and bourbon. Beat until mixture is smooth; about 2–3 minutes.
3. Remove pastry disc from refrigerator and sit at room temperature for five minutes. On a floured surface, roll the dough into a 12-inch round. Transfer dough to pie pan; lightly press the dough into the bottom and sides of the pan, using your fingers. Be careful not to stretch the dough. Trim and crimp edges, using a fork or your fingers. Pour sweet potato mixture into unbaked pie crust and smooth the top. Bake for about 35–45 minutes, or until center is set and crust is golden brown. Allow to cool completely before serving.

Recipe Tip: To roast sweet potatoes, wrap each potato in foil and place on a cookie sheet. Bake in a 375°F oven for 1 hour and 20 minutes, or until potatoes are fork tender. Cool for 10 minutes before making pie filling.

— makes —

8 to 10 servings

Active Prep: 1 hour

Inactive Prep: 30 minutes

— ingredients —

2–3 medium sweet potatoes, roasted and peeled (about 2 cups)
2½ tablespoons unsalted butter, softened
1½ teaspoons cinnamon
½ teaspoon nutmeg
½ teaspoon salt
¼ cup granulated sugar
½ cup light or dark brown sugar, firmly packed
1½ teaspoons vanilla extract
2 eggs
⅓ cup milk
1 teaspoon grated orange zest
½ teaspoon lemon juice
2 teaspoons bourbon (optional)
Single Crust Pie Pastry, unbaked (see recipe)

COOKIES AND BARS

Bourbon Pecan Bars
Cherry Rugelach
Chocolate Chip Cookies
Chocolate "Cracklers"
Fudgy Brownies *(Variation: Turtle)*
Jam Thumbprint Cookies
Limoncello Bars
Oatmeal Cranberry Cookies
(Variation: Oatmeal Raisin)

Bourbon Pecan Bars

These bars take the traditional pecan pie one step further. The tender, buttery shortbread combined with a rich, chewy pecan topping makes for a heavenly dessert. Drizzle melted chocolate on top to make them super decadent.

makes

2 dozen bars

Active Prep: 1 hour

Inactive Prep: 30 minutes

Shortbread

1. Preheat oven to 350°F. Spray a 9" x 13" baking pan with cooking spray, then line the bottom with parchment paper. Set aside.
2. In a medium bowl, sift together flour, baking powder, and salt. Set aside.
3. In an electric mixer on medium speed, beat butter and sugar in a large bowl until light and fluffy, about 2–3 minutes. Add eggs and vanilla extract and mix until well combined. On low speed, add in the flour mixture just until a soft dough forms. Transfer dough to prepared pan. With lightly floured hands, press dough evenly into bottom of the pan. Bake for about 15 minutes, or until crust is set but not browned. Set aside to cool.

ingredients

- 2¼ cups all-purpose flour
- ¼ teaspoon baking powder
- ¼ teaspoon salt
- 1¼ cups unsalted butter, softened
- ½ cup granulated sugar
- 2 eggs
- ½ teaspoon vanilla extract

Pecan Topping

1. In a large saucepan, combine butter, honey, brown sugar, bourbon, orange zest and salt. Cook on low heat, stirring with a wooden spoon, until butter has melted, about 2–3 minutes. Raise the heat to medium high and let mixture come to a boil. Still stirring, allow mixture to boil for 3–4 minutes. Remove from heat and stir in half-and-half and pecans.
2. Pour mixture over prepared crust. Bake for about 20–25 minutes, or until filling is set in the center. Allow to cool to room temperature. Place chocolate in a small bowl. Microwave on high for 1 minute, or until chocolate is almost melted. Remove from microwave and stir until chocolate is completely melted and smooth. Lightly drizzle melted chocolate over top of pecan bars. Refrigerate until chocolate is firm. Cut into bars and serve.

- 1 cup unsalted butter
- ¾ cup honey
- 1¼ cups light or dark brown sugar, firmly packed
- 4 teaspoons bourbon
- ½ teaspoon grated orange zest
- ¼ teaspoon salt
- ¼ cup half-and-half
- 2 cups pecans, coarsely chopped
- 4 oz. semisweet chocolate (optional)

Figure 1

Figure 2

Figure 3

Cherry Rugelach

My version of these traditional Jewish cookies produces a tender, flaky pastry paired with a sweet and tart cherry, raisin and walnut filling. If you prefer, substitute the cherry preserves with any fruit flavor you like.

1. In a small bowl, sift together flour and ½ teaspoon of salt. Set aside.
2. Using an electric mixer on medium speed, beat cream cheese and butter in a large bowl until light and fluffy, about 2–3 minutes. Add in vanilla extract and ¼ cup of sugar; mix until well combined. With mixer on low, add in flour mixture just until combined and a soft dough forms. On a floured surface, form the dough into a ball. Divide dough into 4 equal parts. Shape each ball into a 5" x 5" square, and wrap each square in plastic wrap. Refrigerate until dough is firm, up to 24 hours.
3. To make cookies, preheat oven to 350°F. Line two baking sheets with wax paper, parchment paper or a silicone baking mat. Remove one piece of dough from the refrigerator. On a floured surface, roll out dough into a rectangle, about 12" x 8" *(Figure 1)*. Transfer to a sheet of parchment paper and place back into the refrigerator to chill while rolling out the remaining three pieces of dough in the same manner. In a small bowl, combine 6 tablespoons of sugar, remaining ⅛ teaspoon of salt, brown sugar, 1 teaspoon cinnamon, nutmeg, raisins, and walnuts. Set aside.
4. Remove one sheet of dough and place on work surface, with a 12-inch side facing you. Using an offset spatula, spread ¼ cup of preserves evenly on dough. Sprinkle ½ cup of sugar mixture on the dough, pressing it in lightly with your hands. Using the parchment paper to help you, roll the dough tightly into a log and place on prepared baking sheet *(Figure 2)*. Prepare the three remaining pieces of dough in the same manner. In a small bowl, combine the remaining 2 tablespoons of sugar and 1 teaspoon of cinnamon. Brush logs with egg wash and sprinkle with the cinnamon sugar mixture. Using a sharp knife, slice each log into 12 cookies *(Figure 3)*. Place cookies onto baking sheets. If dough is too soft to cut, chill logs in refrigerator for 20–30 minutes until firm again.
5. Bake for about 25–30 minutes, or until cookies are a light golden brown. Transfer cookies to a cooling rack to cool completely. Store cookies in an airtight container in between sheets of wax paper.

— makes —

4 dozen cookies

Active Prep: 2 hours

Inactive Prep: up to 24 hours

— ingredients —

2 cups all-purpose flour

½ teaspoon salt, plus ⅛ teaspoon

1 8-oz. package cream cheese, softened

1 cup unsalted butter, softened

1½ teaspoons vanilla extract

¼ cup granulated sugar, plus 8 tablespoons

¼ cup light brown sugar, firmly packed

2 teaspoons cinnamon

½ teaspoon nutmeg

1 cup raisins, chopped

1¼ cup walnuts, finely chopped

1 cup cherry preserves, pureed in blender or food processor

egg wash (1 egg beaten with 1 tablespoon milk)

Chocolate Chip Cookies

An old favorite, these soft and chewy cookies are filled with chocolate chips in every bite. Bake them 1 or 2 minutes longer if you prefer a crunchier cookie. Store at room temperature in an airtight container.

makes

3 dozen cookies

Active Prep: 30 minutes

Inactive Prep: 10 minutes

ingredients

2½ cups all-purpose flour
1½ teaspoons baking soda
½ teaspoon salt
¾ cup unsalted butter or margarine, softened
¾ cup granulated sugar
¾ cup light brown sugar, firmly packed
2 eggs
2 teaspoons vanilla extract
1½ cups semisweet chocolate chips
1 cup chopped nuts (optional)

1. Preheat oven to 350°F. In a medium bowl, sift together flour, baking soda, and salt. Set aside.

2. Using an electric mixer on medium speed, beat butter, granulated sugar and brown sugar in a large bowl until light and fluffy, about 2–3 minutes. Add in eggs and vanilla extract and mix until well combined. Add in flour mixture until a soft dough forms. Fold in chocolate chips and nuts.

3. Drop two tablespoons of cookie dough about 2 inches apart on an ungreased cookie sheet. Bake for about 7–8 minutes or until edges are a light golden brown. Transfer cookies to a cooling rack to cool completely.

Figure 1

Chocolate "Cracklers"

These cookies get their name from the coating of powdered sugar that "cracks" as they bake, revealing the soft, fudgy cookie inside. Be sure to use a good quality bittersweet or semisweet chocolate.

makes

3 dozen cookies

Active Prep: 1 hour
Inactive Prep: up to 12 hours

ingredients

1 ½ cups all-purpose flour
½ teaspoon salt
½ teaspoon baking powder
4 tablespoons unsalted butter
2 tablespoons hot brewed coffee
8 ounces semisweet or bittersweet chocolate, coarsely chopped
½ cup granulated sugar
2 eggs
2 teaspoons vanilla extract
2 cups powdered sugar

1. In a medium bowl, sift together flour, salt, and baking powder. Set aside.
2. In a small glass bowl placed over a large saucepan of simmering water, combine butter, coffee, and chocolate. Stir with a wooden spoon until chocolate is melted, and all ingredients are well combined. Remove from heat and set aside to cool slightly.
3. Using an electric mixer on medium speed, beat sugar and eggs until pale and fluffy, about 4–5 minutes. Add in vanilla extract. Stir in melted chocolate mixture by hand until well incorporated. Add in flour mixture and combine until just incorporated. Be careful not to overmix. Cover dough with plastic wrap and refrigerate until firm, at least 1 hour. Dough can be refrigerated overnight.
4. To make cookies, preheat oven to 325°F. Line baking sheet with wax paper, parchment paper, or a silicone baking mat. Sift powdered sugar into a large shallow bowl.
5. Remove dough from refrigerator. With lightly greased hands, shape dough into 1-inch balls. Roll each ball in the powdered sugar until completely covered and no chocolate shows though *(Figure 1)*. Place about 2 inches apart on cookie sheet. If dough becomes too soft, place it back in the refrigerator to chill until it becomes firm again. Bake cookies for 10–12 minutes, or until the edges are slightly firm but the centers are still soft. Transfer cookies to a cooling rack to cool completely.

Fudgy Brownies

These easy-to-make brownies are a chocolate lover's dream! Although the recipe calls for walnuts, you can use any type of nut you like.

1 dozen brownies

Active Prep: 1 hour

Inactive Prep: 30 minutes

ingredients

⅔ cup, plus 1 tablespoon all-purpose flour
¼ teaspoon baking powder
¼ teaspoon salt
1 cup walnuts, coarsely chopped
2 oz. (about ¼ cup) semisweet chocolate, chopped
2 oz. (about ¼ cup) unsweetened chocolate
½ cup unsalted butter
1 cup granulated sugar
2 eggs
1 teaspoon vanilla extract
1 tablespoon instant coffee powder

1. Preheat oven to 350°F. Lightly spray an 8" x 8" pan with cooking spray.
2. In a small bowl, sift together cup of flour, baking powder and salt. Set aside. In another small bowl, toss walnuts and semisweet chocolate pieces in remaining 1 tablespoon of flour. Set aside.
3. In a medium saucepan, melt unsweetened chocolate and butter over low heat. Once melted, remove from heat and stir with a wooden spoon until thoroughly combined. In a small measuring cup, combine sugar, eggs, vanilla extract, and coffee powder. Add sugar mixture to chocolate mixture and stir until just combined. Stir flour mixture; be careful not to overmix. Fold in ¾ cup of the nuts and semisweet chocolate. Pour batter into prepared pan and smooth the top. Sprinkle remaining nuts and semisweet chocolate on top; press lightly into batter with hands. Bake 30–35 minutes, or until center is set. Cool completely in pan before cutting.

Turtle Fudgy Brownies (variation): Replace walnuts with pecans, and prepare batter as directed above. Before placing in oven, drizzle top with ¼ cup of warm caramel sauce. Bake as directed.

Recipe Tip: For best results, do not overmix the batter.

Jam Thumbprint Cookies

These elegant shortbread-style cookies are moist with just a hint of lemon. Any flavor of jam or preserves will work well; raspberry is my favorite.

makes

2½ dozen cookies

Active Prep: 2 hours

Inactive Prep: 2 hours

ingredients

2½ cups all-purpose flour
¼ teaspoon salt
1 cup unsalted butter, softened
¾ cup granulated sugar
1 large egg, plus 1 egg yolk
3 tablespoons grated lemon zest
1 tablespoon lemon juice
8–10 tablespoons fruit jam or preserves
powdered sugar, for sprinkling

1. In a small bowl, stir together flour and salt until well combined. Set aside.
2. Using an electric mixer on medium speed, beat butter and sugar in a large bowl until light and fluffy, about 2–3 minutes. Add whole egg, egg yolk, lemon zest, and lemon juice. Beat until well combined. With mixer on low, add in flour mixture, ½ cup at a time, and beat just until a soft dough forms. Transfer dough onto a lightly floured surface and gather into a ball. Wrap dough in plastic wrap and refrigerate until chilled, at least 1 hour.
3. To make cookies, preheat oven to 350°F. Line baking sheet with wax paper, parchment paper or a silicone baking mat. Remove chilled dough from refrigerator. Shape into 1-inch balls, and place 2 inches apart on cookie sheet. If dough becomes too soft, place back into refrigerator until firm again. Using your thumb, make a deep indentation in the center of each ball, creating a small well *(Figure 1)*. Fill each well with about 1 teaspoon of jam *(Figure 2)*.
4. Bake for about 15–17 minutes, or until cookies are firm to touch and light golden brown on bottom. Transfer cookies to a cooling rack to cool completely. Once cookies are cooled, lightly sprinkle with powdered sugar and serve.

Recipe Tip: Instead of using your finger to make the indentations in each ball of dough, you can use the bottom of a ½ teaspoon. Lightly tap the bottom of the ½ teaspoon in flour and press into the center of each ball.

Figure 1

Figure 2

Limoncello Bars

These luscious lemony treats are the perfect blend between sweet and tart. Store any leftover bars in an airtight container in the refrigerator to keep their freshness.

makes

18 bars

Active Prep: 1 hour

Inactive Prep: 3 hours

ingredients

2 cups plus 3 tablespoons all-purpose flour
⅔ cup powdered sugar, plus more for sprinkling
¼ cup cornstarch
1 ¼ teaspoons salt, divided
12 tablespoons unsalted butter, chilled and cut into cubes
4 eggs
1 ⅓ cups granulated sugar
2 heaping teaspoons grated lemon zest
¾ cup lemon juice
⅓ cup whole milk
2 tablespoons limoncello, or any lemon-flavored liqueur
powdered sugar, for dusting

1. Spray a 9" x 13" pan with cooking spray. Line pan with one sheet of parchment or wax paper, then spray again with cooking spray. Lay a second sheet of parchment or wax paper crosswise over the first. Make sure the sheets are slightly higher than the sides of the pan, as this will help you remove the bars from the pan once they have finished baking. Set pan aside.
2. In a large bowl, combine 2 cups of flour, ⅔ cup of powdered sugar, cornstarch, and 1 teaspoon salt. Using a pastry blender or fork, cut in butter until mixture resembles coarse meal. Transfer mixture to prepared pan and press evenly into bottom of pan. Refrigerate for up to 1 hour. Preheat oven to 325°F.
3. Remove crust from refrigerator. Bake for about 20–25 minutes, or until crust is slightly golden.
4. While crust is baking, whisk eggs, granulated sugar, and remaining 3 tablespoons of flour in a medium bowl until mixture is smooth. Add in lemon zest, lemon juice, milk, limoncello, and remaining ¼ teaspoon salt. Mix until well combined.
5. Once crust has finished baking, remove from oven and pour mixture evenly onto warm crust. Place back in the oven and bake for about 20 minutes, or until filling is set. Allow to cool in pan for 20 minutes, then transfer to refrigerator to cool completely, at least 2 hours. Remove from pan by lifting wax or parchment paper and place on cutting board. Sprinkle top of bars with powdered sugar and cut into squares.

Oatmeal Cranberry Cookies

These chewy, hearty spiced cookies never seem to stay in the cookie jar for very long. Great as a lunch-box treat or a quick snack any time of the day.

2½ dozen cookies

Active Prep: 30 minutes

Inactive Prep: 10 minutes

ingredients

¾ cup all-purpose flour
½ teaspoon baking soda
1 heaping teaspoon cinnamon
¼ teaspoon nutmeg
¼ teaspoon salt
¾ cup granulated sugar
¼ cup light brown sugar, firmly packed
½ cup unsalted butter or margarine, softened
1 egg
1 tablespoon vanilla extract
1½ cups old-fashioned rolled oats
1 cup dried cranberries
¾ cup chopped walnuts (optional)

1. Preheat oven to 375°F. In a small bowl, sift flour, baking soda, cinnamon, nutmeg, and salt. Set aside.
2. Using an electric mixer on medium speed, beat granulated sugar, brown sugar, and butter until light and fluffy, about 2–3 minutes. Add egg and vanilla extract. Mix until well combined. Add in flour mixture and blend until a soft dough forms. Stir in oats, cranberries, and walnuts.
3. Drop two tablespoons of cookie dough about 2 inches apart on an ungreased cookie sheet. Bake for about 7–8 minutes or until edges are a light golden brown. Transfer cookies to a cooling rack to cool completely.

Oatmeal Raisin Cookies (variation): Replace dried cranberries with 1 cup of raisins. Bake as directed above.

MUFFINS

Banana Nut Muffins
Cranberry Orange Crumble Muffins
(Variation: Blueberry)
Lemon Poppy Seed Muffins

Banana Nut Muffins

These substantial muffins are full of flavor and spice; great for breakfast with a glass of freshly squeezed orange juice.

1. Preheat oven to 350°F. Spray muffin pans with cooking spray or use paper liners. Set aside.
2. In a medium bowl, sift together flour, salt, baking powder, baking soda, cinnamon and nutmeg. Set aside.
3. Using an electric mixer on medium speed, beat butter, granulated sugar and brown sugar in a large bowl until light and fluffy, about 2–3 minutes. Add in eggs and vanilla extract and mix until combined. Add in bananas. Add in half of flour mixture and ½ cup of buttermilk, stirring lightly by hand just until combined. Add in remaining flour mixture and buttermilk; stir just until combined. Batter will be lumpy, so be careful not to overmix.
4. Pour batter into prepared muffin pans, filling each cup about ¾ full. Sprinkle about 1 teaspoon of nuts on top of each cup. Bake 15–20 minutes, or until toothpick inserted in the center of a muffin comes out clean. Remove muffins from the pan and cool on a cooling rack for 15 minutes before serving. Store muffins in an airtight container.

24 muffins

Active Prep: 30 minutes

Inactive Prep: 20 minutes

ingredients

2 cups all-purpose flour
1 teaspoon salt
1 ½ teaspoons baking powder
½ teaspoon baking soda
2 heaping teaspoons cinnamon
¼ teaspoon nutmeg
½ cup unsalted butter or margarine, softened
½ cup granulated sugar
½ cup light brown sugar, firmly packed
2 eggs
2 teaspoons vanilla extract
2 large ripe bananas, mashed (about 1 ½ cups)
1 cup buttermilk
½ cup walnuts, chopped (optional)

Cranberry Orange Crumble Muffins

These tender, light muffins are surprisingly easy to make. Great for breakfast with your morning coffee or as an afternoon treat.

— makes —

18 muffins

Active Prep: 45 minutes

Inactive Prep: 20 minutes

— ingredients —

1¾ cups, plus 1 tablespoon all-purpose flour
2½ teaspoons baking powder
½ teaspoon salt
1 cup granulated sugar
2 eggs
½ cup vegetable oil
¾ cup milk
2 teaspoons vanilla extract
2 cups fresh or frozen unsweetened cranberries
2 teaspoons grated orange zest

½ cup all-purpose flour
4 teaspoons light brown sugar, firmly packed
1 tablespoon granulated sugar
½ teaspoon baking powder
⅛ teaspoon salt
2 tablespoons unsalted butter, melted

Muffins

1. Preheat oven to 350°F. Spray muffin pans with cooking spray or use paper liners. In a medium bowl, sift together 1¾ cups of flour, baking powder, and salt. Set aside. In a small bowl, toss cranberries with remaining 1 tablespoon of flour and set aside.

2. Using an electric hand mixer on medium speed, beat sugar, eggs, and vegetable oil until well combined, about 2 minutes. Add milk and vanilla extract. Mix until well incorporated. With mixer on low, add in flour mixture just until incorporated. Be careful not to overmix. Fold in cranberries and orange zest.

3. Pour batter into prepared muffin cups, filling each cup about ¾ full. Sprinkle each cup with the crumble topping and bake immediately for 25–30 minutes, or until toothpick inserted in the center of a muffin comes out clean. Remove muffins from the pan and cool on a cooling rack for 15 minutes before serving. Store muffins in an airtight container.

Crumble Topping

1. Combine flour, brown sugar, granulated sugar, baking powder, and salt in a medium bowl. Stir in melted butter with a fork and combine until mixture resembles pea-sized crumbles. Set aside.

Blueberry Muffins (variation): Replace cranberries and orange zest with 2 cups of fresh or frozen unsweetened blueberries. Bake as directed above.

Recipe Tip: If you prefer crispier edges, omit the muffin liners and spray the muffin tins with cooking spray.

Lemon Poppyseed Muffins

These light and lemony muffins are such a delightful treat! A perfect snack for any time of the day.

1. Preheat oven to 375°F. Spray muffin pans with cooking spray or use paper liners. In a medium bowl, sift together flour, baking powder, baking soda, salt, and poppy seeds. Set aside.

2. Using an electric mixer on medium speed, beat butter and sugar in a large bowl until light and fluffy, about 2–3 minutes. Add in eggs, one at a time, until well incorporated. Mix in vanilla extract and lemon zest. In a small measuring cup, blend together yogurt and lemon juice. With mixer on low, add the flour mixture and yogurt mixture alternately until just combined, starting and ending with the flour mixture. Do not overmix.

3. Pour batter into prepared muffin cups, filling each cup about ¾ full. Bake for about 20–25 minutes, or until toothpick inserted in the center of a muffin comes out clean. Remove muffins from the pan and cool on a cooling rack for 5 minutes. While muffins are still warm, brush glaze over muffins and serve. Store muffins in an airtight container.

— makes —

18 muffins

Active Prep: 45 minutes

Inactive Prep: 10 minutes

— ingredients —

3 cups all-purpose flour
1 tablespoon baking powder
½ teaspoon baking soda
½ teaspoon salt
2 tablespoons poppy seeds
¾ cup unsalted butter, softened
1¼ cups granulated sugar
2 eggs
2 teaspoons vanilla extract
1 tablespoon lemon zest
1½ cups plain yogurt
2 tablespoons lemon juice
Lemon Glaze (see recipe)

Recipe Tip: If you prefer crispier edges, omit the muffin liners and spray the muffin tins with cooking spray.

FROSTINGS, ICINGS AND GLAZES

Apricot Glaze

ingredients

½ cup apricot preserves

1 tablespoon water

1. Place apricot preserves and water in a small saucepan over medium heat. Stir until mixture is fully combined and starts to simmer, about 5-7 minutes. Remove from heat and strain into a small bowl to remove any chunks of fruit. Set aside to cool slightly.

Recipe Tip: You can also substitute the one tablespoon of water for a tablespoon of Grand Marnier or any other orange-flavored liqueur.

Basic Buttercream Frosting

ingredients

4 cups powdered sugar

1 cup unsalted butter or shortening, softened

¼ teaspoon salt

2 teaspoons vanilla extract

2–4 tablespoons milk

1. In a medium bowl, sift powdered sugar. Set aside.
2. Using an electric mixer on medium speed, beat butter or shortening in a large bowl until light and fluffy, about 2–3 minutes. Add vanilla extract and salt and continue to beat until well combined. Add powdered sugar to butter mixture, ½ cup at a time, mixing well after each addition. Stop the mixer to scrape down the sides of the bowl as needed. Add milk, one tablespoon at a time, until frosting reaches a spreadable consistency.

Lemon Buttercream Frosting (variation): Replace vanilla extract and milk with 2 tablespoons of lemon juice and 1 teaspoon of grated lemon zest. Add in 1–2 teaspoons of yellow food coloring if you prefer a stronger yellow color.

Recipe Tip: To produce a slightly whiter frosting, use shortening instead of butter.

Chocolate Frosting

ingredients

1¾ cups heavy cream
¾ cup unsalted butter
½ teaspoon instant espresso powder
6 tablespoons unsweetened cocoa powder
½ cup powdered sugar
¾ cup light corn syrup
¼ teaspoon salt
2 cups milk or semisweet chocolate, chopped
2 teaspoons vanilla extract
¼ teaspoon almond extract

1. In a medium saucepan over medium low heat, whisk together heavy cream, butter, espresso powder, cocoa powder, powdered sugar, corn syrup and salt until butter is melted and mixture comes to a simmer, about 10–12 minutes. Remove from heat and stir in chopped chocolate and vanilla and almond extracts until mixture is smooth. Refrigerate for at about 2–3 hours, stirring occasionally, or until frosting reaches spreadable consistency. Frosting can be refrigerated overnight.

Cream Cheese Frosting

4 cups powdered sugar
1 8-oz. package cream cheese, softened
½ cup unsalted butter or margarine, softened
2 teaspoons vanilla extract
1–2 tablespoons milk

1. In a medium bowl, sift powdered sugar. Set aside.

2. Using an electric mixer on medium speed, beat cream cheese and butter in a large bowl until light and fluffy, about 2–3 minutes. Add vanilla extract and continue to beat until well combined. Add powdered sugar to cream cheese mixture, ½ cup at a time, mixing well after each addition. Stop the mixer to scrape down the sides of the bowl as needed. Add milk, one tablespoon at a time, until frosting reaches a spreadable consistency.

Simple Sugar Glaze

ingredients

1 cup powdered sugar

1 teaspoon vanilla extract

2–3 teaspoons milk

1. Sift powdered sugar into a large bowl. Whisk in vanilla extract and milk, one teaspoon at a time, until icing is smooth and thick. Drizzle over cake.

Lemon Glaze (variation): Replace milk with 2–3 teaspoons of lemon juice and ¼ teaspoon of grated lemon zest.

Orange Glaze (variation): Replace milk with 2–3 teaspoons of orange juice and ¼ teaspoon of grated orange zest.

Toasted Pecan Coconut Frosting

1. Preheat oven to 350°F. Place pecans on a cookie sheet in an even, single layer. Bake for about 8–10 minutes or until pecans slightly darkened. Cool completely, then coarsely chop. Set aside.

2. In a large saucepan, whisk together egg yolks, milk, vanilla extract and sugar until well combined. Add butter and cook over medium heat for 12–15 minutes, or until mixture thickens and slightly darkens. Do not allow mixture to boil. Remove from heat and stir in coconut and pecans. Cool completely. Frosting can be refrigerated overnight.

ingredients

2½ cups pecan halves

4 egg yolks

1 12-oz. can evaporated milk

2 teaspoons vanilla extract

1½ cups granulated sugar

¾ cup unsalted butter

3½ cups shredded coconut

PIE CRUSTS AND PASTRY SHELLS

Single-Crust Pie Pastry
Double-Crust Pie Pastry
Graham Cracker Crust *(Variation: Chocolate)*
Tart Pastry Shell

Pie Pastry

Single-Crust

— ingredients —

1 cup all-purpose flour,
plus more for rolling
½ teaspoon salt
⅓ cup chilled vegetable shortening
or unsalted butter, cut into cubes
3–6 tablespoons ice water

1. In a medium bowl, sift flour and salt. Using a pastry blender or fork, cut in shortening until mixture resembles coarse meal *(Figure 1)*. Add ice water, one tablespoon at a time, just until a ball of dough forms. Be careful not to over-mix the dough. Transfer dough onto a lightly floured surface. Form dough into a flattened disc and wrap in plastic wrap. Refrigerate at least one hour to allow dough to rest.

2. Remove pastry disc from refrigerator and let it sit at room temperature for five minutes. On a floured surface, roll the dough out into a 12-inch round *(Figure 2)*. Transfer dough to an 8- or 9-inch pie pan *(Figure 3)*. Lightly press the dough into the bottom and sides of the pan, using your fingers. Be careful not to stretch the dough. Trim and crimp edges, using a fork or your fingers *(Figure 4)*. Pour filling into crust and bake as directed.

3. FOR PRE-BAKED PIE PASTRY: After transferring dough to pie pan, use a fork to prick holes in the bottom and sides of the crust to prevent air bubbles from forming during baking. Bake in a 350°F for 8–10 minutes or until crust is a light golden brown. Prepare filling as directed.

Figure 1

Figure 2

Figure 3

Figure 4

Double-Crust

ingredients

2 cups all-purpose flour, plus more for rolling
1 1/4 teaspoon salt
2/3 cup chilled vegetable shortening or unsalted butter, cut into cubes
5–8 tablespoons ice water

1. In a medium bowl, sift flour and salt. Using a pastry blender or fork, cut in shortening until mixture resembles coarse meal *(Figure 1)*. Add ice water, 1 tablespoon at a time, just until a ball of dough forms. Be careful not to overmix the dough. Transfer dough onto a lightly floured surface. Divide dough into two equal pieces. Form each piece of dough into a flattened disc and wrap each in plastic wrap. Refrigerate at least one hour to allow dough to rest.

2. Remove one of the pastry discs from refrigerator and let it sit at room temperature for five minutes. On a floured surface, roll the dough out into a 12-inch round if using an 8- or 9-inch pie pan or into a 12" x 15" rectangle if using a 9" x 13" dish *(Figure 2)*. Transfer dough to pie pan. Using your fingers, lightly press the dough into the bottom and sides of the pan *(Figure 3)*. Be careful not to stretch the dough. Pour filling into crust and dot the top with butter.

3. Remove second disc from refrigerator. Roll out the dough into a round slightly larger than the pie pan or dish. Place dough on top of filling. Trim and crimp edges to seal, using a fork or your fingers *(Figure 4)*. Cut 3–4 half-inch slits in top of pie to allow steam to escape. Bake as directed.

Graham Cracker Crust

Figure 1

ingredients

2 cups graham cracker crumbs

¼ cup sugar

½ cup unsalted butter, melted

1. Combine graham cracker crumbs, sugar, and melted butter in a small bowl. Press mixture into desired pan *(Figure 1)*. Set aside and prepare filling as directed.
2. FOR PRE-BAKED GRAHAM CRACKER CRUST: Bake in a 375 °F for 8 minutes. Allow to cool before pouring filling into crust.

Chocolate Graham Cracker Crust (variation): Replace regular graham cracker crumbs with chocolate graham cracker or chocolate wafer cookie crumbs.

Figure 1

Figure 2

Tart Pastry Shell

1. Combine flour, salt, and sugar in a food processor. Add in butter and pulse until mixture resembles coarse meal, about 10 pulses. Add egg yolks to flour mixture and pulse 4–5 more times. Add ice water, one tablespoon at a time, and pulse just until a ball of dough forms. Be careful not to overmix. Transfer dough to a floured surface and form into a ball. Flatten into disc and wrap in plastic wrap. Refrigerate at least 30 minutes to allow dough to rest, up to overnight.

2. Preheat oven to 400°F. Remove the pastry disc from the refrigerator and let it sit at room temperature for 5 minutes. On a floured surface, roll the dough out into a 12-inch round. Transfer dough into a 9- or 10-inch tart pan with a removable bottom. Lightly press dough into the bottom and up the sides of the pan, being careful not the stretch the dough. Roll the rolling pin over the top of the tart pan to remove any excess dough *(Figure 1).* Using a fork, prick the bottom of the dough to prevent air bubbles from forming during baking *(Figure 2).* Bake for about 20–25 minutes or until crust is a light golden brown. Cool completely. Prepare filling as directed.

ingredients

1 ½ cups all-purpose flour, plus more for rolling
¼ teaspoon salt
¼ cup granulated sugar
½ cup unsalted butter, chilled and cut into cubes
2 egg yolks, lightly beaten
3–4 tablespoons ice water

Index